AUGUSTINE BAKER

Frontiers of the Spirit

VICTOR DE WAAL

SLG Press
Convent of the Incarnation Fairacres
Parker Street Oxford OX4 1TB England

www.slgpress.co.uk

AUGUSTINE BAKER

Frontiers of the Spirit

First published by SLG Press, 2010

In memory of Father Wilfred Knox OGS, who introduced me to *HOLY WISDOM* when I first began to try to pray, and for the Sisters of the Society of the Sacred Cross, Tymawr, who live and pray on the frontier.

Cover illustration:

The Temple Church (London), in The Mirror of Literature, Amusement, and Instruction, *vol. 10, no. 274, 22 September 1827. The picture has been selected because Augustine Baker became a lawyer and a member of the Middle Temple. The image is in the public domain because its copyright has expired.*

ISBN   978-0-7283-0181-8
ISSN   0307-1405

Printed by:
Will Print Oxford England

PREFACE

AUGUSTINE BAKER (1575-1641) crossed and lived on several frontiers. Abergavenny, where he was born, is a town on the border between Wales and England, and the boy's first language was Welsh; but so that he could get on in life, he was sent to London to learn English. He wrote in the rich English of the seventeenth century, although the prolixity of his language may have something to do with his Welsh background. He continued to write in Welsh in his private correspondence with Welsh colleagues when he wanted to keep his views hidden from his superiors. His religion also reflects disputed frontiers. His parents and family were Catholics at heart, though his father as a prominent citizen assented to the Reformation Settlement; while the Welsh clergy, conforming to the new Prayer Book, seem to have preserved many of the old ways. Baker himself, fairly typically as a young man at the beginning of the modern age, came to doubt religious faith altogether. That first rebelliousness of adolescence against authority remained with him throughout his life, so that after his conversion he nevertheless remained predisposed to question the Church's authorities, and especially the received teaching on the spiritual life. In the Renaissance tradition of his time, he pitted his learning of the ancients against the corrupt notions of the day. His choice of the monastic life was also itself a commitment to living in a borderland, the frontier between this world and the next, a borderland, however, in which he encouraged all serious Christians, not only monks and nuns, to make their home.

It was no doubt this complex background of many cross-currents, of surviving on these borderlands, that made him the manifestly difficult person that he became, always stubbornly sure of his views, sometimes indeed quarrelsome. Even as a Benedictine monk, he remained an individualist and scarcely a community man. His portrait shows him in the traditional habit, but one wonders how much he actually wore it. He certainly rarely attended choir. His Order came to call him Venerable, but there has never been a move to canonise him as a saint. Baker's writing about the need for a guide in the frontier regions of life is of particular interest today, when the search for a relevant spirituality has become central again for many in the churches and, more significantly perhaps, for those who no longer find their home there. Where may such a guide be found, and how can we be assured of their trustworthiness? How can we test our own insights and discern which path it is best to follow? Of course, much has been written on these themes in the centuries that followed; wisdom has come from the East, and during the nineteenth and twentieth centuries, psychologists have become our respected masters. In our time there is a significant revival of the teaching of St Ignatius Loyola; perhaps, therefore, Augustine Baker's 'Holy Wisdom'—as his first disciples called it—compiled from his writings a generation later than those of St Ignatius, can find its place and become a significant resource for today.

This small study is intended as an introductory guide to Augustine Baker's life and teaching, making use as far as possible of extracts of his writings, so that the reader can hear him in his own words and taste the flavour of his distinctive style.

I am indebted to the late Dame Teresa Rodrigues OSB, who died on 1 February 2010, for wise advice at the outset, and particularly to Sister Avis Mary SLG for much encouragement and skilful editing.

VICTOR DE WAAL
London, April 2010

iv

I

I begin with five pictures in the mind's eye. They are pictures of a life, because, as with all spiritual masters, their life's experience is integral to their teaching. So it was also for Augustine Baker.[1]

Born in 1575, he was baptised David, named not after the patron saint of Wales, but after his uncle and godfather, David Lewis. In the first picture, he is one of a group of small boys. The year is about 1580 in the reign of Elizabeth I. They are playing by a river near their home in Abergavenny. The game (which now we call 'Pooh Sticks') is to throw sticks and float paper boats above a little bridge and watch them drift underneath, then retrieve them and do it again. Little David leans over too far and topples in and is in danger of drowning. His companions cry out in alarm, *hubihubi* (the English word 'hubbub' stems from the Welsh). By fortunate chance a man on horseback is crossing the bridge at that moment, jumps down and pulls the child to safety.[2] He is a friend of the family, one of those who gathers with a group of friends at the house of the boy's father to sing together, a favourite Welsh pastime then as now. In his autobiography, Baker tells of encountering this man twenty years later, who had by then become a beneficed clergyman. He also reflects on his own lack of singing skill, which on the one hand made for humility and on the other hand excused him as a monk from the choir office, leaving him more time for prayer in private.

His father was a devout man, attached to the old religion, but because he was a prominent citizen, Steward of the Lordship of Abergavenny, a Justice of the Peace and Sheriff of Monmouthshire, he had to accept the Elizabethan establishment in outward observance. However, he was in the habit of walking in his garden, reading the Latin prayers from his

Primer. Such people were labelled 'Church Papists' at the time. On his deathbed, at the age of seventy-seven, he was reconciled to the Catholic Church by his son. But that is to anticipate. Baker wrote, in fact, that the actual practice of the new religion did not seem at the time all that different to ordinary people in Wales, no doubt because the service was conducted in much the same way and, if in English, it was as strange to them as the Latin. Moreover, he quotes a scornful remark of a Bishop of Llandaff that there was not much religion west of Chepstow!

David was the youngest of thirteen children; the eldest was also a son, the others girls. His mother was the daughter of a Vicar of Abergavenny, where, it would appear, before the Reformation a married priesthood was respectable. Her brother, Doctor David Lewis, was a judge in the Admiralty division, Member of Parliament for Monmouth, and later first Principal of Jesus College, Oxford. At his death he was to leave his godson a sufficient income to support him for the rest of his life. The legacy included a house in the town, which Baker kept in case, as he said, he was turned out of his monastery and needed somewhere to lay his head. A Lewis cousin was to become a Jesuit martyr.

As a child of three, David had smallpox and was not expected to live, but made a remarkable recovery. He went to school in what had before the Dissolution been a Benedictine Priory, but at eleven he was sent to follow his brother to Christ's Hospital School in London to learn English, witnessing on the very day of his arrival the bonfires lit to celebrate the execution of Mary Queen of Scots. The Headmaster of Christ's Hospital and his wife were good Protestants, a loving and prayerful couple who taught the scriptures to their pupils, and this later stood the monk in good stead.

After school, aged only fifteen, as was not unusual in those days, David entered the university in Oxford to what was to become Pembroke College, possibly with a view of qualifying for the 'Protestant' ministry. In his autobiography, he describes himself in the third person as gentle and kind to others, not given to drink or tobacco, and a good student. Curiously, he discovered an affinity between the Welsh and Greek languages. However, after a good beginning, he began to lead an unruly life and guiltily experimented with adolescent sexuality. So after two years his father, wanting him to settle down, summoned him home, although he had not taken his degree.

When he was twenty-one he returned to London, this time to study law, becoming a member of Clifford's Inn and later of the Middle Temple. He wrote that he became so keen that he took his law books to the theatre in case he was bored. As this was the age of Shakespeare, one could wish that he had left some records of what he saw! He was again summoned home on the death of his elder brother to help his father in his legal responsibilities, and he became Recorder of the Borough. There had already been talk of marriage and a church living, both of which, as he was to say later, providentially came to nothing. So much had he given up the practice of his religion by that time that he could not remember the words of the Lord's Prayer at his brother's deathbed.

The second picture is twenty years later. The year is 1600, and the child of our first picture is now twenty-five. Again he is on a bridge, and this time he is himself on horseback, absorbed in musing about the course of his life. The bridge is narrow and the river is in spate. The horse takes fright and refuses either to go on or turn back. David comes to himself, and for the first time in years begins to pray. 'If ever I get out of this danger, I will believe that there is a God who hath more care for my life and safety than I have had of his service and worship.'[3] Somehow he finds himself safe; it is a moment of conversion.

The third picture quickly follows. He had been as good as his word on that fateful bridge, and immersed himself in reading and study of the Christian faith. This led him to be received into the Roman Catholic Church in 1603, and two years later to take the further step, with two Benedictines he had met in London, to travel to Italy, where on 27 May 1605 he entered the novitiate of St Justina's Abbey in Padua and was given the name of Augustine. It was the feast day of Augustine of Canterbury. (Ironically this saint had not been beloved by the bishops of Wales, who resisted his claims of jurisdiction over them.) While the monastery belonged to a Benedictine reform movement, its strong tradition of prayer and meditation was tempered by moderation, a typically Benedictine spirit that informed Baker's later teaching. His fellow novices made him welcome. They came from good Italian families and urged him to sample the community's twenty or so wines to see which he liked best!

In spite of this, both his physical and spiritual health suffered; the former because of a troubled digestion, the latter because he found he could not practise the prescribed meditations. His inability to meditate on the life of Christ, as particularly taught by the Jesuits at this period, at first resulted in his giving up mental prayer altogether for a long time; later it significantly informed his insistence in his teaching that many are called from the outset of their spiritual path to progress rapidly to the imageless prayer of the will. He returned home just in time to be at his dying father's bedside, and then, in London again, to put his lawyer's training at the service of the enterprise of reconstituting the English Benedictines. An aged and long-imprisoned monk, Dom Sigebert Buckley, who had survived from the Abbey of Westminster re-established under Queen Mary, provided the tenuous link with the pre-dissolution monasteries.

The next twenty years, during which the persecution of Catholics was somewhat muted, were productive for Baker, both interiorly during two extended periods of reading in the mystical writers while he was living with two notable recusant families in the country, and also exteriorly in his research in the great libraries of England. He co-operated with the leading historians and antiquaries of the day, Camden and others, and this labour resulted in the publication of the massive *Apostolatus Benedictinorum in Anglia* (Douai, 1626). It was at this time that he was ordained to the Catholic priesthood in Rheims. The year is now 1613, and this particular picture is a little out of focus, because we know nothing of what led up to this step, or what preparation, other than his own reading, had led him towards it. Although known as a priest, he continued in his legal profession, apparently with distinction. We do know that he was then in a state of profound spiritual desolation and believed that 'Holy Orders would remedy his case and recover him'.[4]

The year 1624, however, does come sharply into focus, for the fourth picture finds Augustine Baker at the beginning of the years in which he produced the work for which he is still widely remembered. In that year, at the age of forty-nine, he was asked to help in the formation of a newly-founded community of young nuns at Cambrai in the Spanish Nether-lands, as part of the restoration of English monastic life, perforce at that time on the continent. There were nine of them, high-spirited teenagers from English Catholic families, among them Gertrude More, great-granddaughter of Thomas More. Three older sisters from another convent in Ghent were put in charge, and Baker undertook to introduce them to the Benedictine balance of discipline and contemplative prayer which he had himself learned from his years of study and his often painful struggles in prayer since his own novitiate twenty years before. Over the next nine years he introduced them to, and commented on, the treatises of the mystical tradition and wrote much on his own account. These survive in MS copies, some in Cambrai's successor, the Abbey of

Stanbrook, and are only now being edited by John Clark and printed in full. In 1657, after Baker's death, his disciple Fr Serenus Cressy made a digest of his writings, and published them under the title of *Sancta Sophia (Holy Wisdom)*.[5] This has remained ever since a resource, not only for monastics, and not only for Catholics, but for Christians of every persuasion. In fundamental ways, though deeply traditional, the teaching went against some of the prevailing trends of the time. Baker's orthodoxy was challenged, and although he was vindicated, the controversy and his disagreements with the Chaplain, Fr Francis Hull, resulted in his leaving Cambrai in 1633. He spent the next years at St Gregory's, Douai, (now Downside Abbey) where seminarists, among many others, resorted to him. Finally, and surely unnecessarily, he was sent back on the English mission. It is there in London that we have the fifth and final picture.

This fifth picture is in the year 1641 and Augustine Baker is lying sick in lodgings near his beloved Inns of Court, possibly with the plague which was then raging in London. He has had to move frequently to elude the pursuivants, for the persecution of Catholics, especially priests, has been virulently revived. In fact his fever probably saved him, for the agents were deterred by fear of the plague, and he died on 9 August. He therefore escaped martyrdom in a year in which no less than eighteen priests were executed. He was buried in St Andrew's churchyard in Holborn. His grave is unknown, for when Holborn Viaduct was constructed in the nineteenth century, many burial places were disturbed and remains re-interred elsewhere.

II

Vera Effigies Ad: R: Patris
AVGUSTINI BAKER,
Ætatis 66, Anno Domini 1641.
I nothinge Am. Have nothinge, nothinge Crave
But IESVS, he redeems, all els enslave *Ias. Huffs. Sculpsor*

I nothinge Am, Have nothinge, nothinge Crave
But JESUS, he redeems, all els enslave

The motto under the portrait is a quotation adapted from the Parable of the Pilgrim told by Baker in *Holy Wisdom*, after Walter Hilton's *Ladder of Perfection*, which provides a remarkable parallel to Bunyan's *Pilgrim's Progress*.[6]

Following on from a conference to commemorate the fourth centenary of Augustine Baker's conversion in 1600, a collection of essays was published under the title *That Mysterious Man.*[7] The phrase is taken from verses by Fr Leander Norminton OSB, later in the century, himself the chaplain at Cambrai, and prefixed to the original edition of *Sancta Sophia*, facing a portrait of the author.

On the Picture and Writings
of the late venerable
F. AUGUSTIN BAKER

In Sable lines laid o'er a silver ground
The face of that mysterious Man is found,
Whose secret life and published Writings prove,
To Pray is not to talke, or thinke, but love.

No streame of Words, nor Sparkes of Wit did fill
His tongue or fancy when he Pray'd: His Will
Through Beames diuine, conceived a chast Desire,
And Teares of Ioy enlivened the soft Fire.

Yet some have falsely thought his sober flame
With those Wild-fires that haunt our Isle, the same.
So Idolls to Church-pictures like may be,
And fondest love resemble Charity.

Hayle Booke of life! Temple of Wisedome, hayle!
Against the Synagogues of Hell prevaile.
England may now her SAINT-SOPHIA boast:
A fairer too, then that the Grecians lost.

(The last two lines, of course, refer to the great Church of Sancta Sophia—Christ identified as the Wisdom of God—in Constantinople, which became a mosque when the city fell to the Turks in 1453.)

'Mysterious' in this context has a double resonance. There was certainly something hidden about him, in spite of the autobiographies and the hundreds of thousand of his words that have come down to us. It is only by implication that we can glimpse beneath the contemplative face of his portrait, the eyes gazing inward, the inner secrets of his soul, and that because, as he would himself insist, God's presence there in all of us is beyond words or images. But secondly, he may rightly be called mysterious because of his unrivalled familiarity with the teaching of the Christian mystics, the Fathers and monastic masters of early centuries, not least Cassian and Benedict, and the writers particularly of the Western medieval tradition. In line with the anonymous author of the *Cloud of Unknowing*, which he made available and commented on at length for his young nuns, his 'secret life and published writings prove, to pray is not to talk, or thinke, but love'.

Some passages, both from the copies made of his own manuscripts and from the digest *Holy Wisdom* give a flavour of his writing, both of his style and of the substance. His language is rather repetitive, but we must remember that this is in fact a condensation of spoken lectures; and if it seems somewhat paradoxical that it could be said of him that 'no streame of words, nor sparkes of wit did fill his tongue or fancy', that was of course not when he lectured but when he 'pray'd'.

He wrote chiefly for monastics, but he insisted that the substance was applicable to all Christians who take their calling seriously. He addresses himself to those who in his terminology are called 'seculars', that is

> [those] that live[s] a common life in the world, of what sex or condition soever (for with God there is no difference or acceptance of persons), to whom the Divine Spirit shall have given an effectual call to seek God in these internal ways of contemplation, yet so as that they do not find

themselves obliged to forsake a secular profession and to embrace a religious life (of which state, the person perhaps married or otherwise hindered, is not capable, or, however, finds no inclination thereto), such a soul may make benefit also of these instructions, though purposely written for religious.[8]

He goes on to suggest ways in which his instructions are appropriate and may with discretion be imitated with the help of a spiritual director when, as he puts it, God has found one. As might be expected, the emphasis is on a relatively quiet existence, making the best use of precious time, and on a poverty of spirit that sees oneself as steward of one's possessions, being confident (here he quotes the author of the *Cloud of Unknowing*) that God's providence will take care of necessities, and 'if it should happen to be with some scarcity, He will recompense that with feasting their spirits with far more internal and celestial and desirable delicacies'!

Central to his teaching, as indeed to that of all spiritual masters in every tradition, is that prayer and self-discipline of life are integral to one another. For the latter, he uses the old designation 'mortification', carrying with it the unattractive notion of deadening of the senses. In our language, something like 'self-renunciation' seems a happier word, the self here being the superficial ego, as distinct from the deeper true Self.

It is of the ego-self that Baker writes when he says, 'we must renounce and fly from ourselves, that we may draw near unto God; we must destroy self-love in our souls, that so Divine love may be raised and increased in them'. That transformation is effected in the first place through prayer itself, as prayer progressively reveals us to ourselves; and prayer in turn can only grow in depth as our self-love and pride are progressively uprooted. We rightly delight in so many things in life—food and drink, relaxation, conversation, the acquisition of knowledge— but we know also the hazards of greed and over-indulgence on the one hand, and our attachment to our own and others' good opinion on the other.

He illustrates the point in a charming fantasy:

> For the case with us is far different from that it was with Adam during his state of innocency. For then it was no inconvenience, but rather perhaps a help to him, freely to make use of the pleasures afforded him in paradise. Because, though sensual pleasures were to him, considering the exquisiteness of his temper, far more pleasurable than they can be to us, yet his appetite did not so much as desire or wish the least excess; and his spirit was so replenished with divine love that, by admitting of such innocent satisfactions to nature, it rather increased than diminished or interrupted his fervour in tending to God and expressing its gratitude, love, and obedience to Him; whereas we find all the contrary effects, and therefore must take a quite contrary course.[9]

Milton, Baker's near contemporary, says the same in the Fourth Book of *Paradise Lost*, where Adam and Eve enjoy 'connubial love' infinitely more blissful than after the Fall.

In recommending that contrary course, Augustine Baker sets himself firmly against the prevailing customs of his own, and indeed of earlier and subsequent times, of the adoption of self-inflicted, and sometimes extreme, ascetic practices, what he calls 'voluntary mortifications'. He even counsels against the pious advice that, given a choice, one should choose the less attractive (as it might be in the choice of food), and thus live in a perpetually negative mode. On the contrary, he recognizes that in the ordinary course of existence everyone realistically meets,

> all the crosses and contradictions to self-will which by God's providence shall be sent to or upon them; whether such crosses regard external things, as injuries, disgraces, sickness, loss of friends, or of goods, &c., or internal, as aridities, obscurities, inward distresses, involuntary rising of passions, temptations, &. All these must be quietly

suffered, whether they proceed from God or from creatures. If anything pleasing to nature be to be done, as in refections, recreations, &c., or anything displeasing to be omitted, to do or omit such things, not because they are agreeable to nature, but because they are conformable to God's will. By a constant and careful observing of these directions, a devout soul may be brought to a good established state of mortification, and yet withal be left in a convenient liberty and ease of mind to go on cheerfully in internal ways.[10]

Not least must we bear with our own imperfections and accept the humiliation of our failures. Accepting them increases in us the grace of God and disposes us to more perfect prayer in future.

Our duty therefore in our present state, and the employment of our whole lives, must be constantly and fervently to co-operate with divine grace, thereby endeavouring not only to get victory over self-love, pride, sensuality, &c., by humility, divine love, and all other virtues; but also not to content ourselves with any limited degrees of piety and holiness, but daily to aspire, according to our abilities assisted with grace to the perfection for which we were first created.[11]

He has down-to-earth advice especially for his monastic hearers, and betrays from time to time a certain irony in setting out the necessary virtues and pitfalls of communal existence. To avoid distractions, do not meddle in things that do not concern you. Because we value our independence, it is much harder to submit to others for the love of God than to submit oneself immediately to God himself. We learn patience to cope with anger, with anxiety, with depression. Solitude and interior silence can be practised in the midst of a busy life (for there are always those who, being cut off from the outside world, are constantly writing and answering letters giving advice, asking for news!). Above all, 'Keep thy cell, saith an ancient holy Father, and thy cell will teach thee all things'.

> A soul that by using at first a little violence shall bring herself to a love of this solitude, and that shall therefore love it because there she may more freely and intimately converse with God, it is incredible what progress she will make in internal ways.

But typically he continues:

> Now to the end that solitude may in the beginning become less tedious and afterwards delightful, religious persons not only may, but ought to, preserve a convenient and discreet liberty of spirit about their employments and entertainments of their minds in private, prudently using a variety in them, changing any one, when it becomes over-burdensome, into another more grateful; sometimes reading, sometimes writing, other times working, often praying; yea, if they shall find it convenient, sometimes remaining for a short space in a kind of cessation from all, both external and internal working, yet ever being at least in a virtual attention and tendence to God, referring all to Him and His glory.[12]

Such teaching, though Baker's contemporaries needed reminding of it, was unexceptionable. Yet there was opposition, as Fr Leander's verses testify:

> Yet some have falsely thought his sober flame
> With those Wild-fires that haunt our Isle, the same.

The reference is to the sectaries of the time, who pretended to privileged illuminations, and to the condemnation of Quietism. Baker's writings were examined and he was entirely vindicated. But if we consider the following passage, it becomes clear why his teaching caused anxiety, going as it did, and indeed still does, against the controlling grain of ecclesiastical authority.

> In all good actions, and especially in the internal ways of the spirit which conduct to contemplation and perfection, God alone is our only master and director; and creatures, when He is pleased to use them, are only His instruments.

So that all other teachers whatsoever, whether the light of reason, or external directors, or rules prescribed in books, &c, are no further or otherwise to be followed or hearkened to, than as they are subordinate and conformable to the internal directions and inspirations of God's Holy Spirit, or as God invites, instructs, and moves us to have recourse unto them, by them to be informed in His will, and by Him be enabled to perform it, and if they be made use of any other ways, they will certainly mislead us ... And it may reasonably be believed that the principal ground and reason why true spirituality is in these days so rare, and why matters go so amiss among souls that pretend to aspire to contemplation, is because the most necessary duty of observing, and following divine inspirations is either unknown or wilfully misunderstood, and suspected (if not derided) by some who, in popular opinion, are held and desire to pass for chief masters in spirituality.[13]

III

Baker writes that two basic dispositions may be distinguished in people, the active and the contemplative, while in every person there is a degree of both. Both indeed aspire 'to a perfection of union in spirit with God by perfect love', but their preferred ways of prayer and discipline will differ. The former

> inclines them much to busy their imagination and to frame in their minds motives to the divine love by internal discourse, so that without such reasoning and use of images they can seldom with any efficacy raise or fix their affections on God. Such dispositions are not patient of much solitude or recollection more than shall be necessary to enable them to produce and maintain a right intention in outward doings and works of charity, to which they are powerfully inclined. And proportionately hereto the divine love and union produced by such means is very vigorous, but less pure and spiritual, apt to express itself by much sensible devotion and tenderness.

Granting this, and recognizing that many will probably begin their Christian way in this mode, Baker insists that this is not so in every case, especially among the less educated, which in his day generally meant women. And he protests with some anger at spiritual guides who know no other methods and hold back their pupils from advancing further and more deeply. He may in this be reflecting on the way such teaching contributed to his own long period of spiritual aridity. He continues therefore to write of the other main disposition, the contemplative, as follows,

> Others are naturally of a propension to seek God in the obscurity of faith, with a more profound introversion of spirit, and with less activity and motion in sensitive nature, and without the use of grosser images, yet with far greater simplicity, purity and efficacy. And consequently such

15

souls are not of themselves much inclined to external works (except when God calls them thereto by secret inspirations, or engages therein by command of superiors), but they seek rather to purify themselves and inflame their hearts in the love of God by internal, quiet, and pure actuations in spirit, by a total abstraction from creatures, by solitude, both external and especially internal, so disposing themselves to receive the influxes and inspirations of God, whose guidance chiefly they endeavour to follow in all things. By a constant pursuance of such exercises, their spirits become naked and empty of all strange affections, images, and distractions, the Divine Spirit only lives and operates in them, affording them light to perceive and strength to subdue self-love in its most secret and, to all others, imperceptible insinuations; and by consequence they attain unto an union with God far more strict and immediate than the former. [14]

As part of his teaching Augustine Baker introduces the young nuns to the *Cloud of Unknowing*, a copy of which he had procured for them. In doing so he engagingly tells his own spiritual autobiography, writing in the third person in the manner of St Paul.

I knew a Man, that had a great desire to be Spirituall. For want of a better, I forsooth was his Master or Directour. We lived together, & indeed were never asunder, & So I had good Commodity to know how it went with him, & he was very open to me, So far as his Case was intelligible, & with his Good leave I shall make the same known unto you, So far as I Can Call to mind, Conceive & expresse it, that ye may See the Varietyes and Strangenesses of Spirituall Operations, for some light & instruction in these matters.[15]

For the pulling down of our Schollars Comb, I will & may tell you for a Very truth & for his Confusion (with his good leave be it spoken), that notwithstanding all that Adoe that God seemed to have about him, in guiding him by the said way, that it is somewhat Extraordinary, yet is he as yet in purity & mortification of Soul or Sensuality little or nothing advanced or amended, as all they may Easily perceive that

Converse with him & observe his Cariage & Conversation. God hath done His part with him, but he hath not done his part towards God, nor Corresponded in Life (howsoever he hath done for internall Exercises) to have the foresaid grace and ability, for good prayer & Life received from God. Nevertheless he hath a great hope that God will finally Conclude all those Exercises with a good and profitable Issue, bringing him at length, by means of the foresaid Exercises, to an Exercise of greater Efficacy, the which will more violently draw him out of his manifold imperfections, & in some good measure cleanse him of them ere he part out of this life.[16]

The lack of an external director proved a mixed blessing. On the one hand, he had to pioneer his own way at a time when the old tradition of contemplative prayer was neglected and indeed suspect; to begin with he was 'Masterlesse, yet not without a master … for he had for his Master (as to all matters & directions of moment) the Spirit of God for his interior Director'. On the other hand, his being a 'poor Solitary Scholar'[17] meant that at a critical point in his interior journey he lost his way.

Like Thomas Merton in our own time, he writes of several interior conversions in the course of his life, in addition to his dramatic return to Christian faith as a young man. The first was in the thirty-third year of his age, after he had been 'long at his prayer', when he was briefly granted the grace of 'passive contemplation', only to neglect that gift for lack of guidance, either by a wise director or by reading in the spiritual authors, how to come to terms with the spiritual desolation that invariably follows such a gift.

He had gotten one of his two feet into Heaven, & there might have held & fixed it till he had gotten in the Other foot, & So have made an Everlasting Secure dwelling there, he carelessly 'suffered the former foot to be drawn back, or rather drew it back himselfe, & so lost the fruit of all his former Labours.[18]

17

It was only twelve years later after prolonged study, when he was forty-five, and three years before he was sent to Cambrai, that he was granted what he called his second conversion.[19]

In the matter of necessary mortifications, he tells the sisters (surely with tongue in cheek, for their beloved Abbess is there among them):

Also you may hope to have a Good Crosse Superior if you pray hard for such an One, who shall break & and Contradict your Wills; But such Commodity our Scholar had not, who only had his Master that was as favourable to his Schollar, as he was to himselfe; & and that was favourable enough, for he was a pretty Good Selfe-Lover.[20]

In fact Baker had his own 'contradictions' to cope with, especially his troubled digestion, which for many years not only prevented him from enjoying his food, but left him perpetually hungry.[21]

IV

The difficult question is how to find a trustworthy guide, 'for certainly a guide must needs be had'.[22] Augustine Baker's conviction is the basic tenet, 'by all mystical writers acknowledged', that in this regard 'God alone is our only master and director'. For a 'well-minded' soul he is the guide in the practice of virtue, in the ways of prayer, and indeed in the ordinary decisions of daily life: such actions or omissions, for example, as reading, study of such or such matters, walking, conversing, staying in or quitting solitude in one's cell, taking a journey, undertaking or refusing an employment, accepting or refusing invitations, etc. In all these the bias is towards simplicity and 'liberty of spirit'.

There are three ways in which God's guidance may be sought: the first through a spiritual director, the second by reading, and the third by direct illumination in prayer. It was in what he had to say about the first and the third that Baker made himself unpopular and suspect in his time, whereas it is just these that make him particularly relevant to this day.

As he himself had come to realize on later reflection on the course of his own life, 'the necessity of an external instructor is generally only at the beginning of a contemplative course.'[23] His principal care must be to set them in such a way so that they may not need to have much recourse unto him afterward. Then it is foolish afterwards both to indulge in introspection and repeatedly to go for advice except in real doubt, and the director himself must beware of raising indiscreet questions, for 'the images and internal distractions raised by impertinent consultations about the interior are, of all other, most pernicious ... and destructive to true recollection'. For there is a danger of 'multiplying new perplexities ... one difficulty will be apt to beget a new one', and Baker warns that the peace of mind of both instructor and pupil may well be troubled, and of the 'dangerous familiarities and friendships with such as may prove very unfit counsellors' that may ensue.

On the contrary, knowing that the beginner is likely to be over-scrupulous, the director will encourage a relaxed attitude in matters not of obligation, and above all counsel patience and courage to persevere when the inevitable 'aridities and obscurities' are encountered. These are the difficulties encountered soon after the outset of the spiritual path, what St John of the Cross named the 'night of the senses'. When later Augustine Baker treats of the highest reaches of prayer, he will also speak of the great desolation, the 'dark night of the soul'.

A good director is one who knows 'the degrees of internal prayer', but 'out of humility will not assume unto himself authority to judge of things above his reach'. Most importantly, he must teach his disciples how to 'become illuminated without him, by God alone, by the means of prayer and abstraction of life … wherewith a light will spring forth in the soul far more clear and certain than any that can come from human instructions'. He is to teach them 'how they may themselves find out the way proper to them, by observing themselves what doeth good and what causeth harm to their spirits; in a word he is only God's usher, and must lead souls in God's way and not his own'.

Much more important in a director than learning are 'a good natural judgment' and above all—here he echoes Teresa of Avila's heartfelt plea—personal experience. He quotes the mystic Tauler saying that 'a soul intending perfection ought to seek out an experienced servant of God, though it cost her a journey of many German miles', and he points out that some of the best guides have been 'lay persons and women'. He adds, echoing the insistence of the Desert Fathers, that to such a one, once chosen, it is important 'to deal freely, plainly, and candidly with him, concealing nothing necessary to be known by him'.

V

The second way in which God's guidance may be sought is by reading.[24] 'And this exercise I esteem, for worth and spiritual profit, to be next unto prayer.' Here his own familiarity with the writings of the early Church Fathers through the Middle Ages and down to his own contemporaries comes to the fore. The list set out in *Holy Wisdom* is encyclopaedic and testifies to his own extensive studies during those many years he spent quietly in the recusant households of England. Moreover, as *Holy Wisdom* shows, he made his own what he read, and so was able to make it available to his pupils. Baker refers also at the outset to 'ordinary books, as ecclesiastical history, &c … permitted to souls even in religion to read them for innocent diversion and recreation'.

Considering his own voluminous researches in that subject earlier in his career, he could hardly do otherwise, though now he adds, 'so that be not the principal end, but that the intention further be by such diversion to dispose a weary soul the better afterwards to pursue her internal exercises'. Moreover, again implying his own experience, he recognizes that learning in religious communities had by this time almost taken the place of manual labour. This, of course, was a time before the wealth of literature available in our own day.

However, he is now writing about 'spiritual books': their purpose is not so much to arouse interest as to encourage imitation when and where appropriate, but he warns the reader not to trouble her own brains about anything touching prayer which she does not understand—perhaps in due time she will. In any case, 'mystic writers, in expressing the spiritual way in which they have been led, do often seem to differ extremely from one another'. This is because in such experiences no words are adequate, and they have to invent new expressions and borrow what similitudes from nature they can. 'Generally mystic authors write according to their own experience' as if that were applicable to everyone, 'whereas such is the inexplicable variety of internal dispositions, that the same course and order in all things will scarcely serve any two souls'. Above all, let the disciple not try hastily to apply to herself what she has read, and dangerously and indiscreetly try to imitate the examples and ascetic practices of the saints. Rather, let this be an occasion for humility. As always let her observe her own spirit; otherwise, instead of reaping benefit, it would have been better she 'had never read, nor been able to read any books at all'.

'Voluntary reading must give place to prayer, whensoever the soul finds herself invited thereto.' Be watchful too, if you are enjoying the book very much, that you do not pour yourself 'wholly upon it with an intemperate greediness'. The virtue of mortification may, and sometimes ought, to be practised here also.

However, when all has been said about these two external guides, Baker concludes,

> Yea, I dare with all confidence pronounce, that if all spiritual books in the world were lost, and there were no external directors at all, yet if a soul ... that has natural aptness, though never so simple and unlearned ... will prosecute prayer and abstraction of life, and will resignedly undergo such necessary mortifications as God shall provide for her, observing God and His call exteriorly and interiorly, and so forsake herself, and propose Almighty God, His will, love, honour, for her final intention ... such a soul would walk clearly in perfect light, and with all possible security, and would not fail in due time to arrive at perfect contemplation.[25]

VI

So Baker proceeds to 'the third and principle way by which God teaches internal livers, viz. immediate divine inspirations'.[26]

> The third fore-mentioned, and of all other the most principal means by which God instructs and directs internal livers in the secret paths of His divine love, and upon which depend the two former, are interior illuminations and inspirations of God's Holy Spirit, who is to be acknowledged the only supreme Master.

Classically, Augustine Baker writes of two contradictory forces to be discerned at work in the human psyche—the forces that Paul in the Epistle to the Romans designates 'flesh' and 'spirit', at war with one another. In the Patristic tradition (as for example in the great sermon on the Discernment of Spirits in the *Life of St Antony*), these take on the form of angels and demons (the latter sometimes masquerading in the guise of the former). Ignatius Loyola in his sixteenth century *Spiritual Exercises* calls them simply the good and the bad spirits, and elaborates subtle and psychologically sophisticated rules for their discernment. Baker, himself above all a teacher, significantly calls them 'two internal lights and teachers'. One is the 'new heavenly teacher, the Holy Spirit, freely given us by means of the divine word and sacraments, it being a new divine principle imprinted in our spirits, raising them to God, and continually soliciting us to walk in His ways'. The other is a 'false light, blind and pernicious, a wandering guide', who, if we follow, 'runs into endless errors and labyrinths'.

Steeped in the Rule of St Benedict, Baker begins by quoting the Prologue to the Rule, which begins with the word 'listen' with its implication of 'obey', and, alternating the metaphors, urges that we have our eyes open to the divine light. Benedict 'teaches as himself had been taught' with no other director than the Divine Spirit. His monastery, as a 'school of the Lord's service', is in Baker's gloss, 'a workhouse wherein the art of the Divine Spirit is taught and practised' in all things, and adapted in moderation to the needs of each. Here everyone, silencing the voice of the internal false teacher who raises distractions and unruly emotions, learns to be attentive to the voice of the true Spirit, watchful lest we presume 'to prescribe unto God the ways in which we would have Him lead us'. That way the Spirit is extinguished and we lose our freedom.

How does God communicate his light? We are made in God's image imprinted in us; and, renewed in Baptism, the Eucharist and the Christian life generally, the Holy Spirit infuses all our faculties. This is our buried talent and the seed and the leaven spoken of in the parables of Jesus. Rather like the skills of a poet or musician, the Spirit within us has to be woken into life, stirring into flame 'the grace which before lay in our hearts like coals of fire smothered in the ashes'. In response to prayer, this divine love dispels the mists of self-love, and 'according, therefore, to the measure of charity so is our measure of divine light'. It is this divine gift of discretion that informs the course of our life, even to the point of helping us to plan our day.

Baker realistically grants that for most of us, imperfect as we are, unless conviction comes in an immediate way, and that is unusual, light will often be dim. He therefore sets out criteria by which decisions may be made in cases of doubt, in ways reminiscent again of the rules proposed by Ignatius Loyola in his *Spiritual Exercises*. One is not to waste time if the matter is not important: ordinary reasoning suffices; advice can be sought, impetuosity is to be avoided, especially if the emotions are involved, and an open mind cultivated. He firmly advises against the pious practice of 'praying about it'! This because prayer will be turned into distracting meditation and we may well mistake our own imagination for divine light. 'Discoursing in time of prayer is anything else but prayer', and the matter should be considered before prayer, briefly commended to God, and reflected on afterwards. That way, our understanding may come to be enlightened.

He admits that 'all these instructions and exhortations to attend unto and depend on the divine inspiration would be in vain; yea all the promises of God, that He would give His Holy Spirit to those that pray for it as they ought would be as vain' if we cannot be sure that they truly come from God. Here, and he refers to other spiritual teachers like himself, there can be the assurance of hope rather than the certainty of faith. The tests in brief are: that firstly, we truly endeavour to submit ourselves to the divine will; and subsequently, the confirmation of the good actions and good thoughts that result. Nor, thirdly, will such promptings go against our other obligations, and if those in authority contradict us, then we can be sure that God will make this up.

VII

The final section of *Holy Wisdom* treats comprehensively of Prayer, the ways, stages and difficulties encountered by the Christian who would seriously pursue the inner life of discipleship. In a substantial appendix, Baker suggests 'certain patterns' of prayer.

Drawing undoubtedly on his own experience, not least that of the dead ends he had himself met with earlier, Baker fills out his teaching from his wide reading in the quiet years of his withdrawal in the country. The resultant treatise 'Of Prayer', meticulously assembled by his faithful editor from his voluminous writings, fittingly concludes the book rightly called *Holy Wisdom*.

> Hayle Booke of life! Temple of Wisdome, hayle!
> Against the Synagogues of Hell prevaile.
> England may now her SAINT-SOPHIA boast:
> A fairer too, than that the Grecians lost.

Earlier in the book, Baker gives a charming example of the 'novice's fervour' that characterises the beginning of the spiritual path, and tells a Franciscan story.

> When you are walking at leisure in the market-place thinking of nothing, there meets you a man with a vessel of wine to sell. He invites you to buy it, much commending the excellency of it; and the better to persuade you, he offers you gratis a small glass of it, to the end that, being delighted with the colour and fragrancy of it, you may be more tempted to buy the whole vessel, which you must expect, will cost you very dear. Even so our Lord Jesus ... by a secret inspiration invites you powerfully (instilling a few drops of His sweetness into your heart) to taste how delicious He is. But this is but transitory, being offered, not to satiate or inebriate you, but only to allure you to His service.[27]

26

That is the beginning. The final goal is contemplation, the Vision of God, which may be glimpsed in this life, but perfectly attained only in the next. So Baker traces the way to be traversed.

> The soul aspiring to a perfect union with God, as yet absent, begins with inquiry by meditation; for as St Augustine saith, all good proceeds from the understanding as its first principle. By meditation the soul labours to represent this divine object with all the sensible advantages and motives of admiration and love that it can invent, to the end the will by pure love may rest in Him; but this being done, the will not yet being at free liberty to dispose of itself, is forced with some violence to untwine and withdraw its adhesion from creatures that it may elevate itself and be firmly fixed to this her only goal, and at last, by long custom, the force by little and little diminishing, the object begins to appear in its own perfect light, and the affections flow freely, but yet with wonderful stillness, to it; and then such souls are said to have arrived to perfect mystical union or contemplation. [28]

> But these are secrets of divine love, which, except by experience they be tasted, can in no sort be comprehended. Blessed are those souls that thus lose themselves that they may find themselves! This loss is so infinitely gainful, that it is cheaply bought with all the anguishes of mortification, all the travails of meditation, and all the aridities, obscurities, and desolations attending the prayer of the will. [29]

> There are in a spiritual life no strange novelties or words pretended to. Divine Love is all; it begins with love and there it ends likewise. [30]

Baker concludes, 'Hence it is that some mystic writers do call this perfect union the UNION OF NOTHING WITH NOTHING. [31] Already as a schoolboy, the young David Baker had been in trouble for asserting that God is nothing, which was mistakenly taken to mean that there is no God. This at first sight difficult concept is well expounded by Rowan Williams in his Introduction to *That Mysterious Man*.

> He is careful to guard against the idea that union with God is a cancellation of all that is natural: as he says, it is simply that, in union with God, what makes the soul what it is is just its total and unreserved dependence on God. It is 'nothing' because it is not tied down by any other dependence, nor so marked by its worldly circumstances and preferences that it would cease to be if its supports were taken away. It lives more intensely in this freedom because then the God who is no particular thing, in no particular place, can move and love in it.[32]

But let Augustine Baker have the last word:

> If God, by the means of our prayers, give us the grace and courage to proceed *de virtute in virtutem* (from strength to strength), according to these steps and these directions we shall, without doubt, sooner or later arrive unto the top of the mountain, where God is seen: a mountain, to us that stand below, environed with clouds and darkness, but to them who have their dwelling there, it is peace and serenity and light.
>
> The blessed spirit of Prayer rest upon us all. Amen. Amen.[33]

NOTES

[1] Augustine Baker wrote two autobiographies, one in rhyme; and another more substantial biography was written by his friend and associate Fr Leander Prichard. These are to be found in Dom Justin McCann OSB and Dom Hugh Connolly OSB. edd., *Memorials of Father Augustine Baker and Other Documents Relating to the English Benedictines* (London: Catholic Record Society, 1933). A third spiritual autobiography occurs in the course of Baker's commentary on *The Cloud of Unknowing* in *Secretum*, edited and introduced by John Clark (Salzburg: Institut fur Anglistik und Amerikanistik, 1997).

[2] *Memorials*, 23. see n.1 above.

[3] *ibid.*, 72.

[4] *ibid.*, 98.

[5] *Holy Wisdom or Directions for the Prayer of Contemplation, Extracted of more than Forty Treatises*, By the Ven. Father Augustine Baker, Methodically Digested by the R. F. Serenus Cressy, and now edited from the Douay Edition of 1657 by the Right Rev. Abbot Sweeney, DD. (London: Burns Oates & Washbourne, 1950). More recently Stanbrook Abbey published a version in more present-day English by Dame Teresa Rodrigues, *The Essence of "Holy Wisdom"*, 2001.

[6] *Holy Wisdom*, 58 ff., see n. 5 above.

[7] *That Mysterious Man: Essays on Augustine Baker OSB*, ed. by Michael Woodward, introduced by Rowan Williams (Abergavenny: Three Peaks Press, 2001).

[8] *Holy Wisdom*, 140. ff.

[9] *ibid.*, 203.

[10] *ibid.*, 212.

[11] *ibid.*, 33.

[12] *ibid.*, 227-8.

[13] *ibid.*, 68 & 133.

[14] *ibid.*, 36-7.

[15] *Secretum*, 33. see n.1 above. The spelling is that of the original MS.

[16] *ibid.*, 40.

[17] *ibid.*, 61-2.

[18] *ibid.*, 60.

[19] *ibid.*, 59.

[20] *ibid.*, 48. (Dom David Knowles was surely wrong to see this as a lack of humour.)

[21] *ibid.,* 54-5.
[22] *Holy Wisdom,* 66 ff.
[23] *ibid.,* 74 ff.
[24] *ibid.,* 86 ff.
[25] *ibid.,* 91.
[26] *ibid.,* 92 ff.
[27] *ibid.,* 184.
[28] *ibid.,* 504.
[29] *ibid.,* 546.
[30] *ibid.,* 542.
[31] *ibid.,* 545.
[32] *That Mysterious Man: Essays on Augustine Baker OSB op. cit.,* 8.
[33] *Holy Wisdom,* 546.